DELIVERING THE NEWS

THE HUGH MACLENNAN POETRY SERIES

Editors: Allan Hepburn and Carolyn Smart

Delivering the News

Thomas O'Grady

McGill-Queen's University Press
Montreal & Kingston • London • Chicago

ISBN 978-0-7735-5635-5 (paper)
ISBN 978-0-7735-5827-4 (ePDF)
ISBN 978-0-7735-5828-1 (ePUB)

Legal deposit second quarter 2019
Bibliothèque nationale du Québec

Printed in Canada on acid-free paper that is 100% ancient forest free
(100% post-consumer recycled), processed chlorine free

Funded by the Government of Canada   Financé par le gouvernement du Canada   Canada   Canada Council for the Arts   Conseil des arts du Canada

We acknowledge the support of the Canada Council for the Arts,
which last year invested $153 million to bring the arts to Canadians
throughout the country.

Nous remercions le Conseil des arts du Canada de son soutien. L'an
dernier, le Conseil a investi 153 millions de dollars pour mettre de
l'art dans la vie des Canadiennes et des Canadiens de tout le pays.

Library and Archives Canada Cataloguing in Publication

Title: Delivering the news / Thomas O'Grady.

Names: O'Grady, Thomas, 1956– author.

Series: Hugh MacLennan poetry series.

Description: Series statement: The Hugh MacLennan poetry series |
Poems.

Identifiers: Canadiana (print) 20190047895 | Canadiana (eBOOK)
20190047917 | ISBN 9780773556355 (softcover) |
ISBN 9780773558274 (ePDF) | ISBN 9780773558281 (ePUB)

Classification: LCC PS8579.G735 D45 2019 | DDC C811/.6—dc23

This book was typeset by Marquis Interscript
in 9.5/13 New Baskerville.

for Leah & Brendan

Inniu chuir mé do dhánta,
aoileach, scian, scealláin:
an pháirc mo phár bán,
an rámhainn mo pheann.

CONTENTS

PART TWO   THE WIDE WORLD

DELIVERING THE NEWS

METAPHOR

Stars gasp and die,
dawn's soft black cloth

the hangman's tight-
cinched hood.

      •

At last, before
first light, a way

with words
he understood.

PART ONE

Seeing Red

CONTROLLED BURN

The world had spun, the days grown longer,
brighter, endless winter's dusk-grey snowpack
melted into muddy piles of salt and sand

and gravelly silt, glinting grit. The windows
open wide, the globe a-tilt on the deep-set sill,
we slouched at our high school desks and watched

a rumble of red and ringing gold pull up
and firemen descend from the shining pumper
like a swarm of ragged blackbirds bent

on scouring a close-cropped autumn field.
But this was spring and that field no spreading meadow
of fresh-mown hay but an unkempt urban plot

of tussocky hummocks matted into mangy tufts,
the scraggly fur of an old dog's corpse, ripe
with decay and rot until brought near boiling

by a week of the lengthening sun's low simmer.
And so to stave off random sparks – the flick
of some stray match or a truant's tossed butt –

the captain touched a torch to the tangled mass
and set that clumpy lot ablaze … though not
to let it burn until burnt out of its own accord.

Does nature daydream summer? Minds bored numb
by the dusty white noise squeak of chalk,
the teacher, heedless, yammering on and on,

we sat, the whole room, rapt by the spectacle below
of a shimmering brigade fanned out across that bleak
half-acre: flames licking like crested waves

at knee-high boots, they waded to their ankles
armed not with coiling hoses but with brooms –
stunted Curling Club castoffs, bristles bound tight

as glowing sheaves of Saskatchewan wheat – to beat
that conflagration down to smoldering earth.
We had learned already what happens next:

a night or two of drenching rain and, by the book,
a scorched wasteland sprouts green shoots of life.
The turning world will spawn its own rebirth.

DELIVERING THE NEWS

On wild March days that cotton canvas sack
held rain like a tent and hung so low it thumped

a sodden beat like a leaden weapon sheathed
against my thigh. Schoolboy short, I cinched the strap

up high in a knuckled knot (my collarbone
still sports a phantom bruise) and shouldered on.

From door to door I bore the soggy news,
street by street – Churchill Avenue, Spring Park Road …

•

War, Pestilence, Famine, Death. Was I deaf
to the headline roar of my unwieldy load?

Weight of the world. Art of the backhand toss.
The guileless messenger shot at and missed.

On Friday nights I tallied my receipts
and somehow ended, always, at a loss.

STEERS

Today I walked the shore road
past a field of steers. Swaggering

block-shouldered anvil-browed brutes,
taut muscle and gristle, sheer beef

to the heels … they gave me the eye.
Do heavy-breathing beasts see red

en masse? I returned the stare
through sagging barbed-wire strands

until in phantom fear my knees
went weak and my heart skipped

decades back to that hard lesson
learned in high school hallways –

the bruising jostle and jam
of elbow jabs and hip checks,

slew-foot trip-ups, locker slams …
all life's indignities rehearsed

before the morning bell's
first call. Mere oxen in the sun?

Meekly, I inhaled salt air.
Even a gelded bull has horns.

TWIST

The spitshine on my wine-dark
wingtip brogues a sunburst splash,
a burnished chestnut sheen,

I blink back fifty autumns
to a croaking high noon summons
from a rickety porch, a tarnished

nickel clutched in a knuckly fist:
how that scaresome crone,
her gummy drooling grin

a crooked picket fence
of licorice nibs, stopped me short
in my trudging schoolboy tracks.

How I turned heel and ran,
both ways, to fill her cornerstore
request. How my palm reeked

for days from that scissored snip,
a cud cut from a seeping braid
of tar, wax paper-wrapped:

a gob, molasses-soft, of cured
tobacco ... a pruned "fig"
of Hickey & Nicholson twist.

LAND OF YOUTH

from curve of shore to bend of bay

1   BANK SWALLOWS

Once I lived in trembling fear that a bird's
bright beak would pluck out my eyes – the gravel pit
in Cardigan, my cousins' warning words
the darting shadow of flicker and flit.

Just one peck, I imagined – a heron's quick
ice-pick stab in a pool still rushes to mind –
then behind a scarlet gush of pitch-thick
blood, an empty socket, a lifetime blind.

So egging each other on, we hurled rocks
against the crumbling bank, becoming brave
as Ithacans below those frightening flocks,
each nest-infested tunnel a Cyclops' cave.

What punishment could ever fit that crime?
Once, too, cliff-dwelling swallows swooped this beach.
Now, besieged by the stone-filled fists of time,
they – their spectacle – have soared beyond our reach.

An old album, a thumb-scuffed photograph,
black and white, circa 1964:
centred, hair tied back by a windblown scarf,
my mother in slacks and blouse. "The South Shore."

Behind her, pinned down by stones, a blanket
unfolded across a table-flat, block-
square boulder; and centred there, a basket
holding the Sunday supper. "Picnic Rock."

The trusty Kodak, its accordion case …
My father, trouser cuffs rolled kneecap high –
just picture this – halfway up the cliff's face
to snap that shot with such a focused eye.

How the shutter's blink stops the lapping tongue
of tide and time, the bite of sea on land.
Can a poem's lie keep my parents young?
Words erode into brine-washed grains of sand.

A half hour later rising, or an eyelash
less watchful, and I might have speculated
forever on what brute force could drag or dash
that ton-weight of cold-cast corrugated

steel – a thirty-foot length of corroded
culvert – against our cliff's unsullied base:
What creature's churning gullet had unloaded,
undigested, that rusty carapace?

Instead, I stood defiantly nose-to-nose
with a local farmer (we stopped just a breath
or two short of trading cudgelling blows),
not quite slight David to his Goliath.

More like Jonah in the wake of his rough ride
in the belly of the beast. In the trail
the tractor left – its race against high tide –
I traced the Leviathan's thrashing tail.

Not artesian (from the province of Artois
in northern France), but arterial: a cleft
chipped by nature into the jutting jaw
of the cliff's ruddy face – a cut as deft

and subtle as a surgical incision
(the scalpel's aim true as a bull's-eye dart),
a vein tapped with such pinpoint precision,
straight to the water-table's pulsing heart.

How the day stood still when we sought to quell
thirst's flame on drought-hot afternoons, quaffing
from a mother-of-pearl lined quahog shell
teeth-shivering draughts from that silver spring.

We fancied once the trickle from that rust-
red bluff Ponce de León's Fountain of Youth.
Now, the atrophy of years an ash-like dust,
our fingertips divine the bone-dry truth.

THE GOAL

The lower the cost, the higher the seat ...
Wisdom dispensed by some mountaintop sage?
More like wit that "gallery gods" repeat –
mere common sense – as we plod stage by stage
to the balcony's dizzying nosebleed peak,
our legs paying *twice* the ticketed price
for a breathtaking goal only diehards seek:
the next-to-last row. But dead center ice.
Then – the wonders of daughters, the marvels
of hockey, the magic of rarefied air!
How the worn wool jersey of time unravels
as step by steep step we skip up the stair.
How they become me in their puckish glow,
and I my father forty years ago.

ORNITHOLOGY

1   MOURNING DOVES

For days, every-which-way I go …
mourning doves. Billing and cooing
on telephone lines. Filling trees
like a muted cacophony

of crows. This morning one wooing
pair flew overhead, their lithe wings
scything the bright air into strips
of sound – a flywheel wanting oil.

They make me want to lace on skates
again, for the first time in years:
to scrape that stultifying sheath
of rust from dull, distempered blades

and – scintillating thought! – the love
of my life on my arm once more,
to slice streams of sky-white ribbon
from a sequin-rich sheet of ice.

Projecting its trajectory,
picturing the ball's bright flight –

a lightning streak, an electric
strike across blue sky

toward the flag-staffed
neon flash of green –

I flex, unflex
(wrists loose, hands tight),

and think, improbably,
"pipe-cleaner straight."

In a fairway pond, an egret
waits – a rapt wire, a shock of white.

3 SHAVING OUT-OF-DOORS

I would shave out-of-doors,
my cheeks and jowls scraped
raw as rust on an unstropped blade
dipped quick as frost in a bowl

of barrelled rain; I would risk
that much to learn the name
of the sleep-bedevilling bird
whose strident pitch repeats

those trebling strains that woke
me once, far away: the tritone
squeal of a clothesline wheel –
my mother out greeting the day.

after Louis Le Brocquy's illustrations for The Táin

In time of war,
the Morrígan appears,

her ravenous rush
a calligraphic stroke,

a slick black blur brushed
thick across the page,

an inkspot smeared
to a blotted clot.

•

Death's dark draw:
how I watched, transfixed,

six raucous crows,
their blood-dipped beaks

bright nibs, rip part
from pulsing part a frog,

a tight-closed fist of flesh,
a throbbing heart.

5   CORBIES

Once more, grey light
summons to the fore
that harsh conceit:

Scott's "twa corbies
making a mane."
Who, benighted

by these short, dark days
of March, benumbed
by sheets of rain

and sleet, blankets of snow,
would not concede?
For weeks, a stark,

mirror-imaging pair
of raven-huge blots,
Rorschach-black,

have held forth in that
towering oak a block away
as if holding sway over

lords betrayed by hawks,
by hounds, by ladies fair: every
mortal inch that they survey.

THE OTHER FOOT

This morning, dressing in the pre-dawn light
(or dark … that window when night's curtain parts
and day stumbles in), I wondered can one slight
misstep undo a life – is that how it starts?
Could a wrinkled sleeve in a fumbling grasp
or an unpressed cuff foretell the way we die?
Or those damned darned socks? An unfastened clasp?
A twisted belt? A badly knotted tie?
On hands and knees on the cold closet floor,
I sifted footwear by touch to no avail.
Does history repeat? Our family lore
preserves from long ago a well-told tale
of an early Mass and a mismatched shoe –
one plain-Jane brown paired with one navy blue.

THREE COWS

The morning my brother laid
a rueful hand on that curvaceous
haunch – the sloped fender

of his rumble-seated Dodge
(cash on demand, *finis*) –
my mother saw in that tender

touch, his sad *adieu* to an antique
coupe, her father's kindly thump
(his heavy heart) on their cow's

wide rump, drooping dugs
dried up, as she swayed behind
the tanner's tumbrel cart.

So it happens, time's hard
stroke dealt and felt. My turn
today to slap a broad backside,

a no-longer-limber hip.
Our Springer's pelt a lumbering
Holstein heifer's paint-patch hide,

she looked, a newly weaned pup,
a half-pint calf. We dubbed her,
a dog's life ago, *La vache.*

COLD SHOULDER

Nights when my wife complains of "the cold shoulder,"
shrugging and tugging for, she says, her fair share
of the covers, hanging on for dear life
to the precipitous edge of the bed –
her half halved again – I ask have I told her
of the time I walked three miles in a threadbare
coat … thirty below and the wind like a knife,
my ears almost cut from my hatless head.

Of how I then thawed out each frostbitten part –
mittenless fingers, the tip of my nose –
in the plush-deep warmth of a feline side.
Might this melt even a blanketless heart?
How now another cat, grown chill as the snows,
stakes in old age a claim on the great divide.

FELINE

1   MOUSETRAP

Folk Museum, Toomyvara, Co. Tipperary

Build a better mousetrap,
a wise man said, *and the world*
will beat a path to your door.

A bitter pill for that creature
we found dead last week, a fetal
form on the closet floor,

batted there, we guessed (the rattle
and bang of the night before
explained), by a grey flurry

of unsheathed claw and naked
fang, a lap cat turned tiger
at end of day. But spill no tears

for such a brute demise.
Imagine instead that quaint
contraption in Toomyvara,

the crudest of machines:
a baited box, bottom-hinged for –
surprise! – a scaffold drop

to a water-filled tin …
Would death seem sweeter
by any other means?

The unspeakable shock – not theirs but mine –
of watching, helplessly, a hapless flock
of unfledged goslings wade, a straggling line,
straight into rush hour's low-flying gridlock
from the reedy reaches of Gulliver's Creek;
then, like puffballs pulverized underfoot,
vaporize to powdery spores, a streak
on dry pavement, a downy cloud of brown soot.

Could even the most hardhearted stoic
remain unruffled by a scene like that?
Today, helpless with grief, I prayed for lyric
release as life's last wisp curled from my grey cat.
Let this swell of words be my final stroke:
a verse-blackened page lending weight to smoke.

The typical feature in these cases is that the indeterminacy
is transferred from the atomic to the crude macroscopic level,
which then can be decided by direct observation.
> – Erwin Schrödinger, "The Present Situation
> in Quantum Mechanics" (1935)

Like a cookie tin, she said, and I thought
of fresh-baked shortbread squares … flaky, wafer-

thin layers of sweet dough stacked in a squat
canister bottom-lined with wax paper.

Of fingers prying off an air-tight lid …
the tang of pure uncertainty just before

that first sugary assurance – a candid
whiff of what choice treat lies neatly in store.

Hardly of Schrödinger's tart paradox
(improbable parable of deferred pleasure)

of a cat captive in an infernal box:
"The living and the dead in equal measure."

Her wisdom folly, my ignorance bliss …
that vet's assistant left me much to learn.

Such a quantum leap into the abyss.
Such a simile for an ash-filled urn.

SYNCHRONIZED SWIMMERS

Choreography. Precise
    as minnows darting
side by side through shallows,

shadows: random starts
    and stops, furtive flitting,
lockstep twists and turns.

Then svelte backs arched
    in tandem, tails curled high
like vernal fiddlehead ferns.

PERFECT FIT

Folding each shirt twice,
prolonging my leaving, I spoke
of last night's dream of a dying cat.

Thyroid. Leukemia. Wasting away.
Pathetic. *A grey bag of bones,*
I sighed. She listened,

nodding ... knowing, then lost
in her housecoat hugged me
goodbye. How we try on grief

for size, one sleeve at a time.
No hope she'll survive
the winter, I almost cried.

TALL TALES

This doctor, that nurse … small talk of the ward.
The weather, naturally: "unseasonably cold."
Politics … scandals and scoundrels: none ignored.
The next-door neighbours, their house still unsold.

"So tell me," I started, but should have known
that railroad agent's daughter, country cute,
would sidetrack my question with one of her own:
"Did you drive out via the station route?"

Then down that line she rattled in her bed,
ravelling knotty threads in her father's yarn
of engine bellies scoured – "full steam ahead" –
by four-foot dwarfs in the locomotive barn.

Far-fetched? I laughed till I cried, clutching her hand.
"Grand," she came clean at last. "I'm doing grand …"

MEMORY

Once the crankcase
bearings seized up,

the pedals skipped,
the rear cog slipped,

the gear teeth lost
their grinding grip,

the chain hung limp,
loose links of rust.

HOW IT ENDS

Around and around
the pond

the boatman rows,
back to the bow,

stroke after steady
dripping stroke.

His arms grown heavy,
one oar slips

from its shaky lock ...
and then the other.

•

Leaden-legged,
reversing course at dusk,

the ploughman hangs
a lantern from a pole

above his horse's head.
One false step ...

and that ankle-twisting
dance of body

tumbling softly
into blade-wrought clay.

LETTING GO

Hearing being the final sense to fail,
we huddled together bedside, her breath
growing short, and taking turns told one tale
after another – laughter defying death.

That dark weight about to fall, we plundered
the past but kept it light by holding court
on all those times we gaffed, slipped-up, blundered –
affable give-and-take, our whole lives fair sport.

Odd, though, the letting go of this faux pas:
my stumbling drop of a cumbersome box –
a leaden fridge laid low by gravity's law.
What spared me – *Bumbler! Clod!* – an oaf's hard knocks?

·

"Steady," somebody sniffed – the stiff upper lip.
Lifting her coffin, we strained to keep a grip.

OUTSIDE THE WAKE

We shuffle foot to foot, scuffing our common ground – the
weather ... hockey ... horses ... beer. The evening shadows
lengthen, deepen. Someone sighs. The streetlight blinks
to life. Soon the talk will turn to why we're here.

THAW

April chill: his voice
on my cellphone cellophane
thin, cracking like ice.

WEATHERING

1   HINDENBURG OVER WEST CAPE

after a photograph in the Public Archives of PEI

He squints, mired behind an anvil-shouldered mare. Sodden
air, a clay-cold mass like ash-filled snow, wraps flush around
the leaden sledge, a mud-bound bouldered barge. Below,
beyond where bog-soft headland sedge drops plumb bob like
a stone, a steel-toned dredge of sea, a shelf of molten slate,
delves deep into itself. Above, against a sullen bone-grey sky,
a plate of unwashed delft, a bloated shape – a sudden wind-
blown cloud, a shadow dark as fate, a thumbprint on a brow
grown pale – floats like a whale or an ark.

Once, on a morning
just like this – mid-April,
the clouds giving way
like heavy doors to the first

strong thrust of spring,
a radiant eruption of sun
over foot upon foot
of fresh-fallen snow –

I saw two horses bolt
from a barn like foals
as if they knew that winter
had at long last run

its final lap: as if –
if they could – they would
kick up star-like sparks,
or burst out in song.

Night nuzzles the corn.
For hours, all ears; at first light,
every sense reborn.

It hit so close, that lightning bolt
I dodged last summer, its fiery flash
and jag-toothed crash a muzzleloader's
loud-mouthed shout. I thought
I had been shot.
               But not shot
through and through, struck
to the core, like that old windbreak
birch, a marker for our measured
plot of land. Before it went, it stood,
withstood, for years, beset by blast,
a canker, or a cancer, aimed at trees …
insidious disease. I dodged that too,
the doctor said, his tight-lipped talk
a jolt from the blue.
               "A near miss,"
and yet, like voltage heaven-sent,
it cleared the air and cleared the view.
Let thunder roar. Stunned sunlight pours
on our weed-wild field, floods
gently sloped meadows, drains
down to the whispering shore.

Just our luck. Morning
unloads rain in buckets,
leaden grey. We watch

the sky and wait. We muck
about and pace and place
the day on hold. By noon

we write it off and sigh.
Hours pass. We scoff
at forecasts painted blue.

O ye of little faith! A bold
crow barks a brazen note
of hope behind the barns.

The clouds begin to yield
and lift, pale rays leak through.
Then evening sun erupts.

We walk the lane. Life brightens.
Flooding light weaves braided gold
from a field of sodden grain.

HERMIT CRABS

By noon tomorrow,
    all here receding glance
by rearview glance

at endlessly fading grey,
    mile after multiplying mile,
I'll picture how today – right now,

the tide at lowest ebb,
    the brick-red bars of sand
holding mirrors to the cloudless sky –

my plodding tread perturbed
    in a rippling pool a scurry
of legs, a disembodied

creature carrying home
    upon its back.
I carry mine in my head.

SEEING RED

Blizzard-bound, snowed
under, walled-in ... swallowed
by a whirling world

of white, a mapless maze
of shifting waist-deep drifts,
he wades and wallows.

His hedgerows bent –
though not like ours,
beneath the weight of war

and sorrow ... once more
the winter of our discontent –
he looks ahead as if

to greener pastures.
Hapless cattle lowing
to be fed, he holds his course,

led – as we are too –
by the heartening blaze
of red that frames the doors,

the eaves, the corner trim
of every outlying
Island barn and shed.

ENVOI

Half-past dawn. Croaked awake, we watch the sky
wake too, lead-grey, with the slow lurching launch
of a half-dozen origami cranes –
great blue herons – unfolding from their swaying

pine-top perch above our ruddy rutted lane.
They breast the air, a fleet of tattered flags
unfurling stroke by rowing stroke against
the wave-cresting wind … The morning hours pass.

Noontime comes and goes. The tide ebbs and flows.
We eye the glass-bright bay for fabric hung
on creaking frames of ribs and spine – the flight
of tail-trailing kites let loose and blown astray.

•

Our hearts rise with the sinking sun. Dusk falls.
At end of day, we all come home to roost.

SAILING FROM AN ISLAND

What more could we lose chancing one last glance
at the grey-toned sheet unwinding behind
us where every hill and straight-drilled field slants

to the shore? Look: the whole world seems inclined
to salt at this dim hour – the windbreak pines
along the lanes, sluggish cattle reclined

in huddled herds, rolled haybales stored in lines
against dark barns, all reduced to hazy
shades and forms. See how pre-dawn light refines

away the vibrant reds and greens – that crazy
quilt of midday colour stretched end to end
on this sea-hemmed place. Not for the lazy

or hard-of-rising, or those who would spend
an extra half-morning *at home*, this road
where dipping headlamps redefine each bend

will rise to meet all honouring the code
of catching the day's first boat – bred to gauge
setting out (custom's momentum unslowed

by year upon year of added baggage)
from measureless, meaningless miles away.
Who would forego this true rite of passage –

this rush and race against time's steady sway?

PART TWO

The Wide World

THE RISING

I rose to watch the morning rise
from the dark sloping bay of meadow,
the dark woods below, the dark hills beyond.

Slowly ... *slowly* daybreak's great blue heron
shifted stiffly on its stilted legs. My coffee
sat unstirred, the black pool of night.

I sipped. I sipped again.
I stepped into stillness.
Light lifted into grey creaking flight.

SLEIGHT OF HAND

Next-to-nothingness.
The infinite density of a soul.

A startled starling blown
down the flue's black hole.

Was I a magician pulling
from the empty false-bottom

depths of a stovepipe hat
a scarf that with one quick

flick of the wrist became
a white fluttering dove?

The door swung wide,
I uncupped my hands

and flung out my arms.
The midday sky lit up

in a bronze flash of wings,
a rich scattering splash of stars.

ANDRÉ KERTÉSZ: TWO PHOTOGRAPHS

I

Notice how even a happenstance snap –
Budapest, 1920 ... a couple

peering, utterly rapt, through a knothole
knocked in a fence topped by a tent's striped flap –

draws the mind's wandering eye to focus
on that alluringly unseen swirl spread

beyond the man's straw hat, the woman's scarfed head:
the whirling world of a touring circus.

II

There are none so blind ... Not quite the gospel
truth, but in shutter-stopped time where melody

rings mute as muck-caked streets in Abony
(note those ruts, tumbrel-cut in parallel),

that sightless fiddler, a barefoot urchin
his guiding light, imprints – proof positive –

a candid glimpse of art's imperative:
that we come to our senses, one by one.

CORTONA

The road a comma,
a curving double-clutching
climb to a round plateau,

we paused right there –
halfway to the hill town's
cobbled square – and caught

our breath at the daybreak view
from terracotta rooftop
height. Were we walking

on air? A pure panorama
that sparkling plain below!
Look down, I thought,

and see like mighty gods
the wide world still at rest.
Or else like mere mortals:

looked down upon and blessed.

AU CHAT NOIR (1883)

after Jules Jouy

Last night sat, a cat
  so black and of such size
    that it masked the sun

and even blocked men's eyes
  to the lustrous moon.
    When daylight broke

the cat had slunk away.
  Or was the cat just grey,
    the men just drunk?

BLUE NOTE CATS

1   *BOUNCING WITH BUD*

They could see in the dark.
His fingers. How infidels dance,
feline nimble, a high-tailed prance
on the keyboard's picket fence.

But his mind all thumbs,
a stumble down an alley strewn
with hangdog luck, at breakfast
on the day *Un Poco Loco*

("a little crazy") came to life –
three deftly-struck cuts – he took
a knife to a cat that crossed
his table. And missed

by a whisker. It hissed.
Gone astray, he showed up
hours late for his studio date.
Almost the one that got away.

What might have been.
The night Coltrane dropped in,
Bechet on his brain,
he sat on opportunity's sill

and shot the breeze – the blues,
Prestige and all that jazz …
small talk of the dotted line –
but took his cue from the office

cat who leapt, the window wide,
to find itself swept up
in a purring embrace then placed
in a cab by the curb. Commotion

ensued. No papers signed,
just shouted sheets of sound.
Both tenor and vehicle
slipped off down the street.

No slouch to start,
Monk sat up straight

and took sharp note
when the door blew wide.

Then he played it in stride:
In Walked Bud, as if on cue.

SERGE CHALOFF

Harnessed, yoked, reined in:
    for months, head hung low,
body hitched to pain, anvil-
    dense, I pitied myself …

a horse tethered to a block
    of forge-wrought iron flung
from a wagon's rickety bed.
    How we pull our own weight.

•

Or how it pulls us: last week,
    that photo of a fireman
wrestling with a writhing
    hydranted hose, a one-headed

Hydra gushing spasmodic gasps
    toward the imminent collapse
of all that should not fall …
    But does. Body and soul.

•

Body and Soul. A blue surge
    of song. Baritone sax.
A stooped shouldering of notes
    from the smoldering reed-rough

depths of a Herculean horn ...
  its swelling bell, its brass-
blinkered pads, its serpent's
    neck coiled back upon itself.

•

How we bear our burdens.
  Steeped in dying, the tumor
on his spine a leaden mass, he cut
    his final vinyl wheelchair-bound.

How he purged himself, blowing
    sinuous riff-rich lines ...
Blue Serge. Then "Dead at 33,"
    the morning papers read.

STARS FELL ON ALABAMA

Today, for the first time
in who knows how long,
I put on Cannonball blowing
one of our old songs –

or *tunes* (we never really
learned the words); a thousand
times before I'd heard
those breathtakingly rounded

lines, Adderley at his abandoned
best, until I had every scratch
on that worn disk by heart:
though not like this –

not with an ear so utterly
alert to how the ballad touch
plays true to life's little drama
raised to a perfect pitch.

My heart beats like a hammer now
for what so wordlessly endures:
the slow dance of our romance
through the twist and shout of years.

MYTHOLOGY

1 THEY ALL LAUGHED

Imagine vulgar Vulcan hammering
two-fisted in his forge, muttering "Venus,
Mars … ," his genius a spite-fired furnace
sputtering, his twisted tongue stammering.

Razor subtle, his knotted cords of discord …
rage-wrought wire netting, binding as a buckle.
Yet, once embedded, we heard the gods chuckle
one by one. Then the entire heavens roared.

What if I had succumbed to some gaudy
Gorgon's will-withering get-hither gaze
and thus whiled away the rest of my days
a sculpted hunk … just one more hard body?

O Andromeda! O scandal of scandals …
the way, rockbed-bound, you thrashed in the clutch
of wave after wave, summoning my soft touch:
O Perseus, come in wingèd sandals!

By day I dream of life's dozen labours,
my Herculean hazards: the push-and-pull
of Hydra-headed crowds; the usual bull
(load after massive load); the smiling neighbour's

Dog of Death; and – truly colossal in length
and breadth – ungirdling sturdy Amazon thighs.
By night, tossed and turned, uplifted to black skies,
I, Antaeus, cry: "*Mother ...* give me strength!"

4   (let's take it) nice and easy

Down that rutted road again, our fast-track route –
fleet Atalanta, flat out, setting the pace,
brash Hippomenes giving mad-dash chase,
rationing (gifts from Venus) gilt globes of fruit.

Then – as always, bittersweet! – that aftertaste
of bridled bits beasts gnaw and gnash against …
just desserts hand-picked by a goddess incensed:
lush laurels trimmed with the pitted spoils of haste.

How dared we, dear, go so against the grain,
grafting to your pure basswood trunk – that straight shoot –
my knotty oak … bole and branch, burl and root?
Were we – Philemon, Baucis – daft? Or vain?

Or just plain blessed by the gods' delightful whims?
None but guests from above could yield us this:
out standing in love's bright field, our bower of bliss,
each year's new growth more than a tangle of limbs.

AT McNELLO'S

Hard men. Punters. A thirst for the ponies.
I nursed my pint in the shadows and watched

their equine faces rise then fall as they watched
the Newmarket card play out, race by race,

and, true to form, maligned an afternoon
misspent on a slate of boldly misplaced

wagers: It's My Time, Slip Sliding Away,
Sovereign Debt … top tips turned to also-rans.

•

Hope. The longshot we ride blinkered every day.
Just ask that loveblind lad behind the bar.

Run ragged, pillar to post, he liked his odds
phoning bets to the bookie's coy daughter.

"A good-looking voice." He rang up again.
"Tell us her name, boys." She had him haltered.

TIME WAS, WHEN I SPORTED

from the Irish

Time was, when I sported
fine-spun spools of flaxen hair,

not this coarse, bare-pated
sprouting, a grey-cast field.

Far better to yield thick
raven-black tresses than

to comb patchy headlands
for a sparse ash-grey harvest.

For now no more courting
comes my way, no women

won by old charms; tonight
my thinning hair is *grey* –

not how it one time was.

Time was …

AFTER Ó BRUADAIR

1   PREROGATIVE

Duty demands it, so just
    for the record, I'll venture
this gambit, have a word
    with the bride. Like mother,
like daughter, sweet blooms
    on soft branches, fair's fair
for the poet where customs abide.

Even flim-flamming shysters
    she greets with forbearance;
to thimblerig chancers she grants
    tribute too. Furtive glances
disclose here's my turn
    to be forward: verses tickling
her fancy, I'll ask for what's due.

Thirst troubles my task,
    this plowing alone –
in time of abundance
    that tool lay unknown.

Now bruised to the bone
    by a clay-laden blade,
my fingers grow numb
    on the haft of a spade.

Abandon any hopeful homeward glance:
the bolted gates deny a mother's prayers,
defy a father's curses and the stares
of boys behind his back. Some books by chance
I salvaged for the road: a Euclid worn
from study; Ovid, Virgil, and the Greeks;
and also our St. Columcille, who speaks
of future honour for his race. For scorn
from scholars huddled by a hedge, I teach
the art of life; a ruined poet, now
a spoiled priest, I talk in tongues and bow
my head: *O sing in me, Muse!* I beseech.
When flaming spirit fails to heal my flaw,
I fall: *usque ad necem, uisce-beatha.*

AN SLATÓIR

Avondale, PEI

Harvest time. The high blue skies of August. The land aglow
with gold. His brothers grown into two tall oaks, straight and
true, the third son slouched in their shadow thrown along
the field's red edge. Would this be the year? The old man
coughed, his body bent like a bleach-dyed windbreak pine.
He pointed. "You and you," he said. One brother took his
seat in the jiggling rig, the other took the mare's compliant
blinkered head. "And you …" He knew that nod. He knew
his lot. He took up his rod. His lowly job to hold erect the
grain before the mower.

DÁNTA GRÁDHA

1 ULYSSES

Awake I dream
myself at home
and you away.

The ocean's gash
healed over
to a garish scar,

you nurse love's ache,
a throbbing longing
tender to the touch.

I weave and unweave
words. You gaze
across the crested waves.

I wonder could you
miss me half as much.

Blindfolded. Handcuffed.
Stripped of rank ...

You are my country.
Back to the wall,

this white square
pinned above my heart,

I stand to face love's volley.
Its steady ready aim.

Its singing sting.
And not one shot a blank.

Dublin 2010

AFTER PETRARCH

Sí travïato è 'l folle mi' desio …

The folly of desire leads me astray.
    I follow in your tracks – my plodding pace,
your light and nimble weave – along the rock-
        strewn switchback trail of Love. I swallow dust.

I spur my trusty steed to surer paths –
    I dig my heels and slap and tug the reins.
To no avail. The more I goad his flanks
        the less he heeds. Love steers his stumbling steps.

•

His lather up, he strains against my will
    until I bend then break and come uncinched,
a deadweight bucked by his unbridled gait.

At last we halt where blooming laurel yields
    its bitter fruit: no heartsore bruise to heal,
others flinch and grimace at that tart taste.

Elkhorn Ranch, Arizona

RED AND GREEN

d'après Chagall

Il a promis
qu'ils peindraient
la ville
en rouge, et puis
il a rougi.

Ils l'ont rendue
plutôt une nuance
de vert,
et aussi presque
à l'envers.

•

ROUGE ET VERT

after Chagall

He promised
they'd paint
the town
red, then
blushed.

They turned it
almost
green instead,
and almost
upside down.

THE FALL

after Émile Goudeau

Admired and despised, reviled,
desired, she turned

on her gypsy heel
and turned both cheeks

on sumptuous surroundings:
Les Orients. She went

for company far beneath
herself and now

pours booze for students
in a cabaret where

I delude myself in brute despair,
brought to my knees

(with four or five *confrères*)
by a barmaid bent

on playing her cold tricks.
Did Samson court Delilah?

My dream falls on the muddy floor.
I follow it there and wallow.

LA TZIGANE

after Apollinaire

The gypsy foresaw
our two lives
crossed by darkness.

We bid her adieu, then
from that pit
bright Hope emerged:

love, clumsy
as a trained bear,
danced upright

at our command,
though the bluebird
shed its feathers

and beggars forswore
their Hail Marys.
We knew full well

that we were damned.
Still, into the street love
pulled us, hand in hand:

all this the gypsy foretold.

PARTNERS

They should be dancing.

They should. They should be cutting
the rug around the room, locked
in step in style in each other's arms.

They should be palm to palm,
hand on hipbone, small of the back.
They should be doing the dip.

They should be eye to eye.
Their world should be the spinning
glitter ball above their heads.

Instead they lace on gloves
and spread the ropes and climb
into the squared circle, dimly lit,

of love gone madly out of whack.
They spar. They feint and parry
and reel across the canvas deck.

Fingers clenched, they launch long
looping jabs meant just to sting.
(They never swing from the heels.)

Some hit the mark. They flinch.
They dodge. They counter toe to toe.
They could be dancing.

They bob and weave around the ring.
Then they clinch.

SMOKE SIGNALS

We shoulder what we can.
The morning sky's red clouds
a warning – *each day aim true* –

I sat astride my two-wheeled steed
and plucked with my mind
the high-strung bow of love.

I knew the trail led home.
What message would I code
that you could read …

and how deliver? My hands
in the grip of braking, steering …
I slung across my back

three long-stemmed roses, cellophane-
wrapped. My heart was aquiver.

ELLIPSIS

Late night, the risen moon in full eclipse,
the heavens extinguished, we lay like sole
survivors of some great tremor, body

by quivering body. Had nobody
felt that quake but us? The apocalypse!
Half-awake, you laughed. Sighed. The sky the soul

of darkness, I heard again a camisole
slip to the floor, imagined a body
bright as Coleman Hawkins' golden horn. Lips

on lips, we played it slow … *Body and Soul.*

BEDROOM SUITE

1 SUNDAY MORNING

The eyelid crack of dawn. The first
blush of light in the east, Aurora

rising ... stretching across the sky.
I blink in bed. On either side,

still dead to the waking world,
a blissful body lies, each curled

like a cat or a wife in the arms of sleep.
They must be charmed. Or blessed.

Strike me blind. What mortal would deny
each seems divine? Deep in a dream,

each twitches now like a goddess, Aurora
rising ... stretching across the sky.

Athena, I thought: the grey-eyed goddess
(musing behind her back) … dressing to kill –
girding skirted loins for a boardroom war –
so that when the mirror said "Make the bed,"
I dreamt my drowsing self Odysseus
endowed with a journeyman joiner's skill,
crafting from an olive trunk shafting the floor
a corner post dowelled for a marriage stead.

Complacencies of a rumpled duvet …
of unplumped pillows … of hand-loomed cotton sheets
(a trireme's billowing sails!) thread-count rich.
Did Olympus frown on Penelope,
or deem undone deeds stay-at-homer feats?
Faithful – boudoir-bound – I wait without a stitch.

"You flatter us either way," she laughs –
    my winsome wife – when, eyeing
        her felicitous form, those alluring
            curves arranged in languidly

mattressed lines of limbs and torso
    defined as if carved out by the razor-
        thin tip of some great creator's
            scimitar-bladed knife,

I pause in mid-arpeggio – O
    the shameless appeal of shapely
        chords … *Misty, Body and Soul,*
        My Foolish Heart –

and, picturing Picasso's linocut
    Woman Reclining and Picador
        Playing Guitar, ask: "Which
            holds up the mirror – art or life?"

Last night, you and I ...
    and *Moonlight in Vermont*
on the radio – turned low –

    that hoary hit from '52 ...
Stan Getz guesting on tenor
    with Johnny Smith, guitar

and sax in a soft sashay
    through a grace-noted grove
of swaying sycamore chords.

    The B side of *Tabu*, I knew,
that tune's up-tempo beat
    more in step with our cast-off

quilt of sultry summer heat ...
    Yet, how like a rendezvous
après-ski – the log-fire blush –

    our slaloming down
the slippery slope of love.
    Did you hear near the ending

that slick arpeggiated schuss?

Later, we'll sweep our rosined bows
across the singing strings and saw out
to the concert-master's measured

baton beat the overture's sweet
curtain-raising strains, the cascading rush
of notes arranged to hush the restless

to the edge of their seats. We'll watch
from our orchestral perch the tent flaps close,
the world reduced to a single shining ring.

•

But now we're cued to the drum major's
silver-crowned mace and locked in marching step
with the leggy stride of the top-hatted man on stilts,

the twirlers' swirling pace, the zoo of jungle cats
caged-in on horse-drawn carts, the slow stampede
of pachyderms on parade. Even our hearts race

at the snare's bright roll. We are the trombone's
slippery slide, the trumpet's golden blare.
The tuba's *oom-pah-oom-pah* brings up the rear.

Vestis virum reddit, she likes to quote
(the Latin tongue a tickle on her lips):
"Clothes make the man." So why not just devote
a diverting hour to her hands-on-hips
appraisal of my mock-mannequin pose,
an all-of-me sizing-up of collar,
chest, waist, inseam – hatband to wing-tipped toes:
mere time well spent, not my last half-dollar.
That I would invest, every red cent,
one aisle over in eye-catching *Lingerie*:
my pleasure to assess and nod assent –
a befitting end to a frivolous spree.
Carpe diem! Tickle me head to foot.
Take no man's measure by a pinstriped suit.

This morning,
sunlight streaming in shafts
           past the bedroom blinds –

too bright … too early – my mind
           drifted back between
 those slanted slats to a steamy

        labyrinth of sheets
and last night's dream of a high-stepping
           stallion bridled, saddled,

straddled, steered through that glowing
           grove in Magritte's
Le blanc-seing … a thinned-out

        first-growth stand
of sturdy oak just turning leaf. The story
           of the autumn of my life?

O that well-heeled damsel – hand in glove,
           reins at the ready, crop
by her thigh – dressed for dressage.

           Piaffe! Passage!

The dedicatory epigraph is the opening quatrain of Irish
poet Michael Hartnett's sonnet "Dán Práta" in his volume
A Necklace of Wrens (Dublin: Gallery Books, 1987).
Hartnett translates the lines thus in "Potato Poem":
"Today I planted poems – / dung, knife, seed: / a field
my page, / my pen a spade." This quotation is reproduced
by kind permission of the Estate of Michael Hartnett and
The Gallery Press.

The epigraph to "Land of Youth" comes from James Joyce's
Finnegans Wake (London: Faber and Faber, 1939).

Hungarian-born André Kertész (1894–1985) was an iconic
twentieth-century photographer.

The bohemian cabaret known as Le Chat Noir flourished in
the Montmartre quartier of Paris in the last two decades
of the nineteenth century. Jules Jouy (1855–1897) was
one of its habitués.

The two poems comprising "Blue Note Cats" derive from
anecdotes about pianist Bud Powell and tenor saxophonist
John Coltrane included in Richard Cook's *Blue Note
Records: The Biography* (Boston: Justin, Charles & Co., 2003).

"Up at Minton's" engages with jazz pianists Thelonious
Monk and Bud Powell at Minton's Playhouse, a legendary
Harlem jazz club.

Serge Chaloff (1923–1957) was the pre-eminent jazz
baritone saxophonist of his time.

McNello's is a pub in Inniskeen, Co. Monaghan, best known
for its association with Irish poet Patrick Kavanagh.

"Time Was, When I Sported" translates an anonymous "lay"
from the gathering of Middle Irish poems known as

Duanaire Finn: The Book of the Lays of Fionn, edited by Eoin MacNeill (London: Irish Texts Society, 1908).

"After Ó Bruadair" translates lines from seventeenth-century Irish poet Dáibhí Ó Bruadair included in *Duanaire Dháibhidh Uí Bhruadair/The Poems of David Ó Bruadair*, 3 vols, edited by John C. MacErlean (London: Irish Texts Society, 1910–17).

Dánta grádha is Irish for "love poems."

Émile Goudeau (1849–1906) was another habitué of Le Chat Noir.

Guillaume Apollinaire (1880–1918) was the foremost French poet of the early twentieth century.

The following poems were written in dedication:

"Blue Note Cats" *for Jay Walton.*

"Envoi" *for Mairéad, Caitríona, and Siobhán.*

"Time Was, When I Sported" *for Fionán.*

"Delivering the News" is dedicated to the memory of Seamus Heaney.

ACKNOWLEDGMENTS

Acknowledgment is given to the following journals in which some of the poems in this book first appeared:

Agenda: "Mythology," "Magritte"

Agni: "Artery," "Cold Shoulder," "Indeterminacy"

Another Book: "Time Was, When I Sported," "Picasso," "Makeover"

The Christian Science Monitor: "Mourning Doves," "Trajectory"

Compost: "Untitled"

Consequence: "Morrígan"

Cyphers: "Sunday Morning"

The Fiddlehead: "Twist," "Bank Swallows," "Picnic Rock," "Leviathan," "Corbies," "Three Cows," "Smoke," "Memory," "Prerogative"

Interdisciplinary Humanities: "Serge Chaloff"

The Nashwaak Review: "Steers," "Sailing from an Island," "At McNello's," "*An Slatóir*"

New Hibernia Review: "Mousetrap"

North American Review: "The Odyssey"

Notre Dame Review: "André Kertész: Two Photographs"

Plainsongs: "Delivering the News"

Poetry Ireland Review: "Letting Go," "Envoi," "Stars Fell on Alabama"

RE:AL: Regarding Arts & Letters: "Two Horses"

The Recorder: "The Goal," "Blast," "Moonlight in Vermont"

The River Review/La Revue Rivière: "Shaving Out-of-Doors," "Hindenburg Over West Cape"

Salamander: "The Other Foot"

Studies: An Irish Quarterly Review: "Maynooth, 1822"